GIANTS
OF THE WORLD

Written by
Osman Kaplan

Illustrated by
Öznur Kalender

12 11 10 09   1 2 3 4

Published by Tughra Books
26 Worlds Fair Dr. Unit C,
Somerset, NJ, 08873, USA
www.tughrabooks.com

Giants of the World

Written by Osman Kaplan
Illustrated by Öznur Kalender

ISBN: 978-1-59784-139-9

Printed by Çağlayan A.Ş. Izmir, Turkey

CONTENTS

Milk-Lined Pocket

Wheee! Wheee! My mother is hopping so fast! I love it when she hops like this. I am so excited; I wonder where we are going now? I really want to know, but I cannot ask my mother right now. Or, dear God, we will stumble and fall. I had better just wait for my mommy to stop.

Whee! Whee! Oh, she is slowing down. I guess we are stopping.

I was right. We have come to a new green meadow in the bush. My mother loves to eat the grass here. I guess she was hungry. She has already started to eat the green grass. I have just stuck my head out of her pouch and am watching her.

But I am not going to get out and eat grass. We kangaroos are born really small, and then we stay in our mother's pouch until we are big enough to get out. God is so merciful that He made our mother's pouch really comfortable for us. Everything we need is here.

When I first came into the pouch I was so tiny that I only measured about one-third of an inch. I am as tiny as a bean. I was like a little feather. At that time none of my organs had developed nor were they functioning. I could not even see. But then I started to grow, and soon I will be really big. Like I said, everything I need to eat is ready in the pouch.

God put some milk teats in the pouch for us. Not just one—four! And the milk that flows out of these teats is not the same. Each one is different, for a different stage of our development; they come in different temperatures and consistencies. We go to the teat that is right for our age. And we never mix them up. Even if we have a brother or sister in the pouch with us, we do not get confused. Everybody goes to the teat that is right for their age. Brothers and sisters share the pouch. God has taught us all that we need to know.

I am all alone in this pouch; I do not have a brother or sister. Right now I am drinking from the third teat. Soon I will move up to the fourth teat. That is how the days pass in here; I am growing all the time. I am going to be a big strong kangaroo like my mother.

My mother told me that my back legs and my tail are going to get really strong. Then I will be able to hop really fast, just like her. That will be great, won't it? God willing, those days will come soon.

Now mother has had enough to eat. I guess we will leave soon. I have already snuggled down into the pouch. Now I am holding tight. Whee! Whee!

IDENTITY CARD

We live in Australia and New Guinea. We can grow to be taller than a man. We weigh between 40 and 120 pounds. Our front legs are short, and our back legs are long and powerful. We have a very strong tail too. We are famous for jumping and for having a pouch. There are four different teats in the pouches. Each one carries milk at a different temperature and consistency. We carry our young in the pouches and this is where they feed and grow. When the young first come into our pouches they measure only one-third of an inch.

An Unexpected Event

This morning something happened that was so exciting and so lovely. Actually, it started out like any other day. The herd was up and out. Some were having mud baths, some were washing, and some were drinking. That is why we came to the watering hole. It was not really difficult finding the watering hole as God created us so that we can catch the scent of water from very far away.

I was drinking water with my mother, like the other elephants. Then we went and lay down in the shade of the trees. That was when my two elephant aunts went rushing towards a grove of trees. I could only stand and stare. One of my aunts was walking with great

difficulty; she struggled until she was behind the trees and out of sight. Of course, I was very curious and had to know what had happened.

"Mommy, what is wrong with aunty? Why did she rush away from the water?"

"Don't worry, dear, nothing is wrong. They'll be back soon. I won't tell you where they went. Let it be a surprise for you." Now I really was puzzled, but at least I was happy that my aunt was going to be all right. I did as my mother said and waited. Do you know what happened next? My aunts came out from behind the trees. They started to walk towards us—and there was a baby elephant next to them! He was so cute. He could not stand up without help. So this was my surprise—now I had a new friend. I was so happy. One of my aunts had had a baby behind the trees, and the other had helped her.

"Did I look like that when I was born?" I asked my mother.

"Yes, you looked just like that. But look at you now. You can do so many things for yourself. You have even learned how to use your ears, tusks, and your trunk properly. You know why God gave us these wonderful instruments, don't you?"

"Yes! When I was really little, I didn't know that my trunk could do so much. But just this morning it has done so many different things for me. I have drunk some water, I have sprayed mud on my back, and I have picked grass and leaves with it!"

"OK," my mother said. "Now use your very special trunk to hold on to my tail and follow me. I am going to teach you how to get water out of the ground with your tusks. That dirt patch over there will be a very good place to learn," she said.

I was so happy that I was going to learn something new. I did as my mother told me, and we went over to the dirt patch. A little bit later, I looked back at the herd and saw my new friend suckling milk from his mother. I guess he has to grow a little more before he can do what I am doing now.

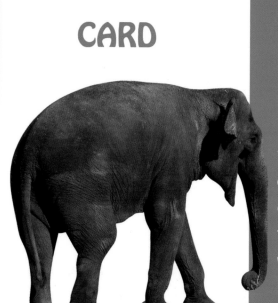

IDENTITY CARD

We live in Asia and Africa. We are the largest of land creatures. We measure up to 13 feet in height, and we weigh as much as 6 tons. We have huge ears and a long trunk. We can do lots of things with our trunk. We eat about 727.5 pounds of plants every day. Water is very important for us. We will sometimes walk miles just to find water. We live for about 60 years.

We Are the Tallest!

It is a good thing I listened to my mother and stayed with her. Otherwise, that big lion would have had me for dinner. But my mother kicked him once with her strong legs, and knocked him flat. Then she got me away from there really quickly.

Now we are going to have some water. But first my mother has to check for lions; she always does that before we drink. If there is no danger, then we can drink. If we were attacked while drinking water, my mother would not even be able to defend herself. Why? Well, let me tell you.

When we giraffes drink water, we cannot defend ourselves. To get our mouths close to the water we have to spread our front legs really wide. Then we can drink, but we would be in terrible trouble if we were attacked because we cannot get up again quickly. Our enemy the lion would not hesitate to attack if he saw us like this. He would go for our neck. So it is very important to look all around before bending down to drink.

Thanks be to God that he gave us a long neck and good eyesight. These help us to see if there is any danger. We can also communicate with our friends. My mother, if she looks carefully in front of her, can see a lion a mile away! Of course, I am too small to do this now. I am still much shorter than my mother.

My mother is nearly 18 feet tall. She can reach the topmost branches on the tallest trees. We giraffes prefer the leaves and flowers of the acacia tree. But we never eat so many leaves that the trees

die out. We eat some and then move on. Soon after we start to eat the leaves, a bitter juice flows from the tree, and when we taste this, we go find another tree. In this way, instead of killing the tree, we simply prune it. When new leaves appear, we go and eat those. It is one of God's mercies that the acacia tree has this bitter juice. How else would we know when to stop eating the leaves? We could kill the tree without even realizing it.

For now, my mother picks leaves and flowers that are too high for me to reach. "You have to eat these if you want to grow quickly," she says. I eat whatever she gives me without fussing; I want to grow as tall as her.

Ah, finally we have come to the watering hole! My mother is checking everywhere. God willing, there is no lion nearby and we will be able to drink our water in peace.

IDENTITY CARD

Reaching up to 16 feet tall, we are the tallest of land animals. We weigh from 2-3 tons. We live in herds in Africa. We love the leaves and shoots of trees and tall bushes. Because of our long legs that can deliver a powerful kick, even the lion is frightened to attack us. We live between 25 and 30 years.

ranched Antlers

"Can you see that tiger over there? He's staring at us."

"Yes, I can see him. I think he is picking out one of the fawns."

"We'd better warn the herd. Stamp your feet quickly!"

"OK. Let's do it together."

After we had warned the herd of the danger, everybody came together. As the leader of the herd, I went to the head. Now we are quickly getting away from that spot; I do not want a tiger to eat one of the small or weak members of my herd.

17

That tiger is far behind us now. Even after he saw me take up the lead of the herd he still tried to chase us. But our legs are strong and we were able to get away from him very quickly. Now we can

If I had been alone, I would not have had to run away from the tiger. My antlers are enough to scare him away. God gave us deer antlers to protect ourselves. But when we are all together as a herd, the safest thing to do is to run to another place. There could have been other attackers hiding among the grass, and if I were busy taking care of one, another could have attacked the herd.

We are very lucky because God gave us strong legs and large, strong antlers. Otherwise, we would have difficulty getting out of dangerous situations. We would be very weak and helpless when we came up against danger.

Our greatest defense is our antlers. They grow again every year. As soon as the old antlers fall off, the new ones begin to come out. Every time we grow new antlers, one more branch is added to them.

While our antlers are growing, they are soft and spongy. They

slow down; the little ones are tired. But we will keep moving until we find a good place to stop.

19

are covered with a soft layer of skin that has veins running through it. People call this skin "velvet" because that is what it feels like. When our antlers have finished growing, the veins break up. We take the dead skin off by rubbing them against trees.

We have run a long way, and now I am really hot. God has been merciful to us. He has made our noses work just like a radiator. When we get too hot, they carry the extra heat out of our bodies. That protects us from overheating.

Ah! Here is a lovely big, green meadow! We will stop here now. We will rest a little and have some of this lovely grass. Oh, that smells good!

IDENTITY CARD

There are many species of deer. We live almost everywhere in the world. Our most important weapon is our branched antlers. We can protect ourselves from enemies with these, even from tigers. But there are many species without antlers. We eat leaves, buds, grass, and shoots. Some species measure up to 6 feet tall. We can weigh up to 485 pounds. Our sight, hearing and sense of smell are all highly developed.

Snowmen

Winter is coming. It will not be long until the babies are born. I had better finish building the den. I have opened a big cavity under the snow; the cold cannot get in there. The thick layers of snow act like a blanket and keep out the cold. Now it is time to make the room where the babies will be born and where I will look after them for the first few months.

It is important that the rooms of the den stay warm. That is why I made the rooms higher than the

entrance to the den. This traps the warm air inside. Newborn cubs cannot stand the Arctic cold.

Polar bear cubs are born very small and without fur. They do not even weigh two pounds and their eyes are not open. I take care of them in the den until springtime. They suckle my milk and grow very fast. Then we all go outside together.

I wonder what the cubs will do when they first see where they live. I remember just staring in amazement at everything around me the first time I left the den when I was little. Everywhere was covered in snow, and the sparkling white of the snow and ice made me blink. When I covered my paws with my eyes, my mother said,

"Don't be scared. God has created us so that we are protected from snow blindness. We have an extra eyelid that looks like a membrane."

I was so happy. I took my paws off my eyes and began to run. And I did not slip at all! I can still run fast over the snow without slipping. My feet are covered with a thick layer of fur. Because of this, I can walk over the snow and ice without slipping and without getting cold.

In fact, it is not only my feet; every part of me is well protected from the cold. God created us perfectly for where we live. From head to toe, every part of us has been created to live at the North Pole.

Our large bodies are covered with white fur. It is very thick, long, and fluffy. It draws sunlight straight into our bodies. This helps our bodies get warm very quickly. Under our skin we have a very thick layer of fat. That helps keep our body heat in. We can swim for hours in icy water without getting cold.

Time has passed quickly. I had better get busy making the rooms. I still have a lot to do. Then I will go fishing for my dinner.

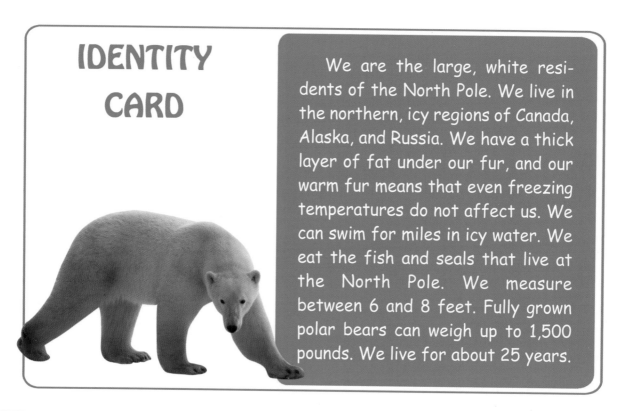

IDENTITY CARD

We are the large, white residents of the North Pole. We live in the northern, icy regions of Canada, Alaska, and Russia. We have a thick layer of fat under our fur, and our warm fur means that even freezing temperatures do not affect us. We can swim for miles in icy water. We eat the fish and seals that live at the North Pole. We measure between 6 and 8 feet. Fully grown polar bears can weigh up to 1,500 pounds. We live for about 25 years.

Underwater Feast

We are going up to the surface again. Oh, I know! It is time to eat! Whenever my mother wants to suckle me, that is what she does. We swim to the surface, and she slows down a little. Then I nurse for a bit. Because I am still little, I cannot stay under the water for very long without breathing. That is why my mother brings me close to the surface a lot, especially when it is time to nurse. Then when I need to, I can easily take a breath.

Of course, as my mother told me, this is only for a while. As I get bigger, everything will get easier. I will take a breath for a minute or two at the surface, and then I will be able to stay for hours under the water. God created us whales so that we can do this easily.

The reason I cannot breathe under water is that I do not have gills like a fish. We have lungs like land mammals. So we have to breathe the air, which means we have to come to the surface. But our lungs are very powerful, and we can stay under water for a long time once we have filled them with air. We can go as deep as we like, and go straight back up again. My mother does this often. She is nursing me a lot so that I grow up quickly and get as big as she is.

Do you know that whales are the biggest creatures in the world? I have aunts that weigh as much as thirty elephants. They are bigger than my mother! Maybe one day I will be like that too!

My mother is swimming and looking at the schools of fish at the same time. She is probably going to come back and eat them when she has finished feeding me. Before she starts to eat, she will probably do what she did yesterday. She made some noises that told the other whales where the fish were.

A few days ago they told us where there was a big school of shrimp. The other whales were really far away, but we could hear them easily, and we found the shrimp right away. My mother loves shrimp, so she was really happy. She and her friends had a great meal.

I think we are nearly at the surface now. I am glad I was able to tell you about all of this before I started to feed. I cannot open my mouth when I am feeding; I have to hold on to the teat and not let go. My mother shoots the milk into my mouth. There are rings of muscles around the teats, and as she tightens or relaxes these muscles she can control the flow of milk into my mouth. If I tried to suck like other mammals do, I would get a lot of seawater in my mouth along with the milk, and that would be bad for me. It is one of God's mercies that He created such an easy and practical way for us to feed.

My mother has slowed down so that it will be easy for me. I guess I should start drinking now.

IDENTITY CARD

We are the biggest creatures in the world. We live in all the oceans and seas. We migrate to warm seas for the birth of our young. We feed on the plankton and fish of the oceans. Thanks to the thick layer of blubber under our skin, we can swim in the coldest seas without any problem. There are quite a few species of whale; the largest is the blue whale. This weighs up to 130 tons and measures 80 feet in length. We have a blowhole on our back. We live between 30 and 200 years, depending on our species.

Confusing Stripes

"We have to put the foals in the middle, right away."

"Is a lion coming?"

"Look up there, in the grass. There are a lot of them. The best thing we can do is to get far away from here."

"Yes, I can see them. You're right. Let's hurry."

My mother and father immediately gave the news to the rest of the herd. Everybody pushed their foals into the middle. My mother pushed me too. Then we all began to run.

My mother is watching me very closely. She is making sure that I run alongside her. She will keep running until we are somewhere safe. This is what we zebras do when we run away from lions. It is not difficult for us to run a long way. God gave us long, strong legs.

We have very powerful lungs as well, so we do not get tired eas-

ily. We can run a long way without getting tired or having to slow down.

God gave us everything we need. We generally live in open grasslands where there is nowhere for us to hide. We can only avoid danger by running away. That is why it is so important for us to be able to run fast.

We have another special feature that protects us without having to run. Do you know what it is? It is the black and white stripes on our body. Often these stripes help protect us from danger without even running away. I have only just learned about these myself. A few days ago we saw a lioness watching us from far away. I went up to my mother right away. I thought we were going to run away, but the zebras in our herd continued to graze. A few of the male zebras got all of the zebras to come closer together. I did not understand what they were doing, and I was a little bit worried about the lioness. My mother had told me that lions were a great danger to us.

So, why weren't we running away? I asked my mother, and this is what she answered:

"Don't worry, dear. If there were any danger, we would have run away. One lioness all by herself cannot cause us any problems," she said.

She looked at my stripes and said,

"Look, you have black and white stripes. When we stand together, the stripes all combine. Any lioness that is looking at us cannot decide which stripes belong to which zebra, and she gets confused. She cannot decide which zebra to attack." This is how I learned why we have black and white stripes.

I am so hungry and thirsty! I hope we stop soon. My mother has already started to slow down. Oh, now I see the grassland ahead. I guess that must be where we are stopping. Hooray! I can eat as much grass as I want. We have left the lions far behind. I bet they are pretty annoyed that they missed us!

IDENTITY CARD

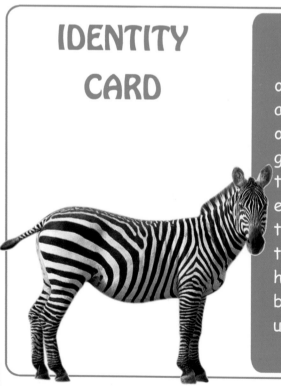

We live in the open grasslands of Africa. We eat grasses, bushes, and shoots. We can run fast in order to escape predators. God gave us long legs and strong lungs to do this. Every zebra has different stripes on its coat, just like the fingerprints of people. We love taking dust baths, and live in herds. While we sleep, some members of the herd keep watch. We usually live for about 25 years.

To Eat and Sleep

I only opened my eyes a few days ago. Everywhere is so pretty. Of course, my mother is the prettiest of all. She is so tender and loving. I love her so much. I have spent most of the time since I was born on her lap. She cuddles me and nurses me. When I get sleepy, she rocks me to sleep.

Of course, the things that happened in the first few days of my life I only felt because my eyes had not opened yet. Pandas are born with their eyes closed. Our eyes open about six weeks after we are born. We are tiny when we are born, about the size of a small rabbit. But, as I was just explaining to you, our mothers look after us so well that we grow very quickly. They give us milk to drink and protect us from danger.

My mother told me that when I am three months old, I will be able to walk all by myself. When I am five months old, I will be able to run and eat bamboo. Did I mention bamboo? I have just learned all about it.

Bamboo is our favorite food. When I am big, I will spend all day eating bamboo, just like the other pandas. When my mother told me about this, I asked her why we spent so much time eating it. I asked her if it was because it is difficult to chew.

"Of course not dear," she said. "Chewing bamboo is easy for us. God gave us strong sharp

teeth to eat the tough outer layer of the bamboo. It takes a long time because we have to eat a lot of it. We have to eat about 90 pounds a day if we want to be full."

A fully grown panda weighs about 264 pounds. So, adult pandas have to eat much to be full.

Those days seem so far away; I am still so small.

While I have been talking to you, my mother has been busy eating bamboo. Now she has stopped eating and is cuddling me. How nice! First, I am going to drink some milk, and then I am going to cuddle her and go to sleep.

IDENTITY CARD

Although we are often called panda bears, we are different than bears. We have black stripes and spots on our white fur. We live in Asia and eat bamboo. We consume about 90 pounds of bamboo every day. When we have finished eating we spend the rest of the day sleeping. A fully grown panda can weigh up to 264 pounds.

Cleanliness and Safety

It has been a long time since I had a good mud bath. The parasites living on me have taken advantage of this, and there are lots of them now. Those little flies and bugs love to make their homes on me. But I do not like them. They make me really itchy.

I will tell the birds to do an extra good cleaning today. Right now I really need it. Ah, here they come! Those birds are great help to us rhinoceroses. They

may be small, but their service is great. It is wonderful that God inspired them to live together with us. Otherwise what would we do? I am sure those pesky parasites would just nibble away at us until they had finished us up. I told the birds what I wanted them to do today.

"Those parasites on my back are really bugging me. All night long I itch all over. Do you think you could get them all for me today?"

"Don't give it a second thought; we will get rid of them all for you. They will do great for our lunch."

"OK. Get started then."

So the birds got started. Right now they are cleaning the parasites off my back. Did you know that the birds do not only clean us; they help to protect us too?

While they are wandering about on our backs, they have a better view of what is going on all around us. If they see an enemy approaching from a distance, they immediately begin to sing. Of course, the song they sing is very different than their normal song. It sounds like they are screaming. In this way we are aware of any danger.

Ah, that's it! As soon as my back is cleaned I am going straight to have a mud bath. I should not have put it off for so long. Almighty God has created mud with so many special properties. There are no bacteria or parasites in mud. So, when we cover our bodies with it, there is nowhere for the parasites to live.

Oh dear, the birds have stopped cleaning and have started to give their alarm. They are screaming now. They must have spotted something. There is a tiger that lives in the forest over there. If he gets hungry, he may head this way. Probably the birds have spotted him. It is a good thing they told me. I must be careful. I would not want anything to happen to my baby. If I need to, I can use my horn to protect her.

IDENTITY CARD

We rhinos are one of the largest animals living on land. We live in India, Africa, and Java. We have a sharp horn on the end of our nose. Because of our size and our horn, no animal dare attack us when we are full grown. We measure about 16 feet long, and weigh up to 3 tons. We eat leaves and grasses, and we love to drink water. We live for about 40 years.

Egg Duty

The ground has become very hot. This heat could harm my eggs. I had better spray some water on them to cool them down. It will not be long before they hatch, and I would hate for anything to happen to them this close to the end.

I am always checking my nest to make sure that nothing happens to them. I check them all the time. I would be very upset if anything were to happen to them. I remember once, a friend of mine came home to find her nest

all smashed up. She was very upset when she saw all the eggs had been broken. I spent a lot of time trying to make her feel better. I would not want to go through the same thing. So I must be careful.

When I made my nest, I spent a lot of time thinking about the safety of my babies. I chose a suitable and safe area, close to the water's edge. That way, I knew that my babies would be able to get into the water easily. Then I brought leaves to build my nest. I dug a big pit and lined it with the leaves and mud that I had brought from the water's edge. Later, I put my eggs into the nest and covered it very carefully.

Now, as I said, I am waiting impatiently for my baby crocodiles to hatch. It is important that I am ready when they hatch because some of the babies might have difficulty breaking out of the eggs. Actually, God has made things very easy for them. While they are still in the eggs, they have sharp, pointy teeth on the end of their nose. These help the babies crack open the eggs. The extra teeth fall off as soon as the babies hatch. But even with this, some of the babies can have difficulty getting out. That is when we mother crocodiles come into play. We help to break the eggs with our teeth. When all the babies have hatched, we put them in our mouth, and carry them carefully to the water's edge. Inspired by God, we help them to get to the water.

Before I started to talk to you about all this, I sprayed my nest with quite a lot of water, but I do not think it is enough. Today is hotter than normal. Maybe I should put some grass on the nest; that will make it cooler. I had better go and get it.

IDENTITY CARD

We look like a giant lizard. We eat the fish that live in the water and animals that approach the water's edge. We live in rivers and swamps. A tough hide covers our bodies. We live for a long time, some species living up to 80 years. Fully grown crocodiles sometimes measure more than 15 feet long. We are different than other creatures in that we open our mouth by raising our upper jaw, not moving the lower one. We live in Asia, America, Africa, and Australia.

The First Race

"Let's race!"

"But how, Mommy?"

"Don't worry, Olly. You can do it! Come on!"

Hearing my mother speak like this made me and my brothers, Otto and Oscar, feel better. We even started running. My mother was right. We could run. And fast! I was in front, and right behind me was Otto. Oscar was last. We ran a long way. Now it was time to turn back to our mother and father.

When we reached my mother, she said,

"Did you see how well you ran? I told you that you would be able to. God gave us ostriches the ability to run fast. All of us can run fast soon after we hatch."

"Mommy! Mommy! When I ran, I used my wings to get my balance," said Oscar excitedly.

My mother said, "Good boy. That is what you should do. That is what God gave us our wings for. We don't use them for flying; we use them for getting our balance when we run."

My mother and father were really happy when they saw us running. My father told us how impatient they had been for us to hatch. They were so happy after they saw our first race. Now we all sat down to rest.

My mother says that we are the fastest two-legged animals. We can go nearly as fast as a car. We also hatch from the biggest eggs.

"You mean that we hatched out of the world's biggest egg?" I asked.

"That's right. The egg you hatched out of weighed nearly 3.5 pounds," my mother said.

She brought over a piece of broken eggshell to show me. She showed us the little holes on the surface.

"Can you see these little holes? That is how you were able to breathe while you were in the egg," she said. "These holes have another very important task. Every egg has the holes in a different place, making it easy for an ostrich to identify its egg."

We were really interested in those holes. We studied them for quite a long time, amazed at the eggshell that we had hatched from.

Now it is time to run again. We are going to race one another. We feel much less worried about running now. We know that we are expert runners.

IDENTITY CARD

We are the fastest runner on two legs in the animal kingdom. We can reach 45 miles an hour. We are 6-10 feet tall, and we weigh between 245 pounds and 350 pounds. We eat green vegetables, grasses, and seeds. We will eat small insects as well. We live in groups, and we put our eggs and chicks into a nursery. Most of us live in Australia. We can eat small pieces of metal and glass. We live between 60 and 70 years.

Water Games

I am yawning so much! When the birds see that my mouth is open, they gather round. I will ask them if they have come to clean it up.

"Hi there, have you come to clean?"

"Yes, when we saw you yawning, we thought we should ask. Would you like us to clean your teeth for you?"

"That would be great, thanks."

I love these little birds. They come often to clean my teeth. The particles that get stuck in this hippopotamus' teeth are enough to fill them up. They are tiny little birds, so they do not eat much. They do not worry about running between my long, sharp teeth. But I would never do any-

thing to hurt them or frighten them. God inspired them to help me. Now I am opening my mouth wide to have it cleaned, and the rest is up to the birds.

It took a long time to clean my mouth, but now the last bird has left. They all flew away together. They looked happy; I guess they were full. Now my daughter Tiny and I can have a nice swim. I am sure she will be happy when she hears that. She loves to play in the water with me. She loves to climb on my back and jump in the water.

Hippos love to swim, and we are very good at it. We can stay a long time under the water. Our Creator made things easy for us here; we close our nostrils when we dive, and then water does not come into our noses.

"Let's swim," I said to Tiny. She was really happy. Now she is climbing on my back for the third time to dive into the water. It is lovely cooling off in the water in this hot weather. But we do not have to worry about burning under the sun. God gave us a special liquid in our skin that prevents it from burning. So even though we have no fur we do not burn.

It is not only heat that does not affect us; cold does not bother us either. Our skin is very thick and there is a two inches layer of fat under it. We can stay warm even in cold water.

Tiny has just seen the crocodiles by the side of the water.

"Mommy, why are those crocodiles staring at us?" she asked.

"You don't need to worry while I am by your side," I said. "But don't forget to always be careful when you see crocodiles."

Crocodiles can really cause us a lot of trouble. They see our babies as easy prey. They know that we adults can fight back with our huge jaw, but we still have to be careful.

IDENTITY CARD

We live in watering holes in Africa. We have no fur. We are herbivores. We have large heads and bodies. We have long sharp teeth in our mouths. We are very good swimmers. When we are adults we weigh up to 5 tons and we can be up to 16 feet long. Because of our huge size and our big teeth even crocodiles think twice about attacking us. We live in herds. We can stay under water for a long time.

At the Beach

We had better hurry up and finish so that we can get back to the sea. I came to this beach to lay my eggs. We sea turtles never come to land except to lay eggs. Male sea turtles never leave the sea. We cannot move as well on land and cannot defend ourselves.

I am going to choose a good place to make my nest on the beach. Then I will open a pit about 20 inches deep there. I will lay all my eggs in it; I usually lay about a hundred eggs, each as big as a ping-pong ball and white. Then I cover them with sand.

I leave tracks behind me when I go back to the sea; these are so that my babies can follow me and get to the sea more easily. I followed my mother's tracks many years ago.

I will never forget the day I hatched. When my brothers and sisters and I had hatched we started to dig our way through the sand. We finally managed to get out. Everywhere was dark, but there was a light shining in front of us. With inspiration from God, we understood on that dark night that the light was where the sea was. Our only goal was to get to the sea. We followed the tracks in front of us. And then we reached the sea. When we got into the sea, we all felt very happy. We began to swim to the open sea in the moonlight.

Of course, this was all years ago. Even though I have traveled very far from here and many years have passed, I had no problem coming back to the place where I was born.

Finally, I have found a suitable place to make my nest. Now I should start digging. I still have one or two hours' work. I have to

get back in the sea before it gets
light.

How lovely! In about two
months my babies will come into

the sea. I will pray for now that they will not encounter any danger.

Once they get into the sea, there is not so much to worry about. When they get a bit bigger, everything is really easy. They grow and grow until they weigh 770-880 pounds. They can swim really fast too, so they do not have many enemies. They eat fish and other sea creatures and continue to grow. For example, up to now I have just been chased by sharks a couple of times; I have not encountered any other dangers. We can hide in our shells, like our land bound cousins. Then animals like sharks and whales cannot see anything to eat other than a shell. But, as I just said, since we can swim fast, getting away from them is not difficult.

Now my eggs are all buried, and my duty is done. I am heading back to the sea.

IDENTITY CARD

We live in the Mediterranean, Pacific and Atlantic oceans and lay our eggs on the beaches. We measure about three feet, and weigh between 330 and 440 pounds. The heaviest of us weigh as much as 990 pounds. We eat sea creatures. We love crabs the best. Only the females go on land to lay eggs, and then they return straight to the sea. The babies run to the sea the minute they hatch. We can live up to 300-350 years.